AF481149

MOMMY GAVE ME MONEY! MONEY BOOK

Math Books for Kids

Children's Money and Saving Reference

HI KIDS!

Let's practice counting money!

MONEY is the most common medium of exchange.

MONEY is used to barter or trade with each other in exchange for the things they needed.

Popular currencies in the world.

- ↳ **Dollar**
- ↳ **Euro**
- ↳ **Yen**
- ↳ **Pound**
- ↳ **Peso**
- ↳ **Franc**

The US dollar is the official currency of the United States. It is also the most traded currency in the world.

COINS CHART

Name	Front	Back	Value
Penny			1 cent 1 ¢
Nickel			5 cents 5 ¢
Dime			10 cents 10 ¢
Quarter			25 cents 25 ¢
Half-dollar			50 cents 50 ¢

BILLS CHART

		1 dollar bill $ 1
		2 dollar bill $ 2
		5 dollar bill $ 5
		10 dollar bill $ 10
		20 dollar bill $ 20
		50 dollar bill $ 50
		100 dollar bill $ 100

WORD PROBLEMS

Directions: Write your answer in the space provided.

EXERCISE NO. 1

Sally has 11 dimes and 5 quarters. All in all, how much money does Sally have?

___

Sara sold lemonade in her neighborhood. She got 7 pennies on Saturday and 12 pennies on Sunday. What amount of money did Sara receive?

___

When Benny was visited by the toothfairy, he received 16 each of dimes, pennies, and quarters. How much money did the toothfairy leave Benny?

___

EXERCISE NO. 2

Jason got 13 pennies and 14 dimes shining shoes, and in his tip jar found 4 dimes and 2 quarters. How much money did Jason get?

On Monday, Melanie spent 3 quarters playing pinball. The next day, she spent 16 quarters on pinball. What was the total amount Melanie spent playing pinball?

While digging through her clothes for ice cream money, Joan found 14 quarters in her pants, and 18 quarters in her shirt. How much money did Joan find?

As Sam was searching through his couch cushions, he found 14 dimes, and 18 quarters in the couch. How much money in total does Sam have?

On Friday, Sally spent 3 nickels on ice cream. The next day, Sally spent 18 pennies on baseball cards. All in all, how much money did Sally spend?

Jessica found 17 nickels, 4 dimes, and 18 quarters in her house, and found 6 dimes in her piggybank. How much money did Jessica find?

EXERCISE NO. 4

When Sandy was visited by the toothfairy, she received 2 each of pennies, dimes, and nickels. How much money did the toothfairy leave Sandy?

____

Sam found 13 pennies, 18 dimes, and 17 quarters in his house, and found 15 dimes in his piggybank. How much money did Sam find?

____

Tom got 2 dimes for washing clothes, and 18 nickels for watering plants. How much money does Tom have?

____

EXERCISE NO. 5

As Joan was searching through her couch cushions, she found 7 pennies, and 13 dimes in the couch. How much money in total does Joan have?

___

Alyssa got 2 nickels and 15 quarters shining shoes, and in her tip jar found 12 quarters and 8 dimes. How much money did Alyssa get?

___

Alyssa sold lemonade in her neighborhood. She got 2 pennies on Saturday and 3 pennies on Sunday. What amount of money did Alyssa receive?

___

EXERCISE NO. 6

On Friday, Sara spent 5 quarters on ice cream. The next day, Sara spent 17 dimes on baseball cards. All in all, how much money did Sara spend?

___

On Tuesday, Jason spent 4 nickels playing pinball. The next day, he spent 13 nickels on pinball. What was the total amount Jason spent playing pinball?

___

Jason has 3 pennies and 2 quarters. All in all, how much money does Jason have?

___

EXERCISE NO. 7

On Friday, Keith spent 3 dimes on ice cream. The next day, Keith spent 15 quarters on baseball cards. All in all, how much money did Keith spend?

____

Sally got 3 nickels for washing clothes, and 12 pennies for mowing lawns. How much money does Sally have?

____

Fred sold lemonade in his neighborhood. He got 6 pennies on Saturday and 11 pennies on Sunday. What amount of money did Fred receive?

____

As Tom was searching through his couch cushions, he found 6 dimes, and 2 quarters in the couch. How much money in total does Tom have?

When Alyssa was visited by the toothfairy, she received 14 each of dimes, pennies, and nickels. How much money did the toothfairy leave Alyssa?

While digging through her clothes for ice cream money, Sally found 7 pennies in her shorts, and 14 pennies in her jacket. How much money did Sally find?

Jessica has 18 quarters and 15 nickels. All in all, how much money does Jessica have?

___

Benny got 16 nickels and 2 pennies shining shoes, and in his tip jar found 8 pennies and 12 dimes. How much money did Benny get?

___

Mary found 14 pennies, 17 dimes, and 4 nickels in her house, and found 18 dimes in her piggybank. How much money did Mary find?

___

As Alyssa was searching through her couch cushions, she found 18 nickels, and 17 pennies in the couch. How much money in total does Alyssa have?

Dan sold lemonade in his neighborhood. He got 4 pennies on Saturday and 9 pennies on Sunday. What amount of money did Dan receive?

Sally found 3 dimes, 8 pennies, and 9 quarters in her house, and found 7 pennies in her piggybank. How much money did Sally find?

Melanie got 16 dimes for washing clothes, and 13 nickels for mowing lawns. How much money does Melanie have?

____

While digging through her clothes for ice cream money, Alyssa found 11 nickels in her pants, and 13 nickels in her jacket. How much money did Alyssa find?

____

Mike got 12 pennies and 14 dimes shining shoes, and in his tip jar found 9 dimes and 17 quarters. How much money did Mike get?

____

On Sunday, Joan spent 18 dimes playing pinball. The next day, she spent 15 dimes on pinball. What was the total amount Joan spent playing pinball?

On Friday, Tom spent 17 pennies on ice cream. The next day, Tom spent 13 nickels on baseball cards. All in all, how much money did Tom spend?

When Benny was visited by the toothfairy, he received 15 each of dimes, quarters, and nickels. How much money did the toothfairy leave Benny?

EXERCISE NO. 13

As Sally was searching through her couch cushions, she found 11 pennies, and 12 quarters in the couch. How much money in total does Sally have?

____

When Tim was visited by the toothfairy, he received 6 each of nickels, pennies, and dimes. How much money did the toothfairy leave Tim?

____

Melanie has 16 pennies and 13 nickels. All in all, how much money does Melanie have?

____

Nancy sold lemonade in her neighborhood. She got 17 nickels on Saturday and 10 nickels on Sunday. What amount of money did Nancy receive?

____

On Wednesday, Dan spent 16 quarters playing pinball. The next day, he spent 4 quarters on pinball. What was the total amount Dan spent playing pinball?

____

On Friday, Sandy spent 3 quarters on ice cream. The next day, Sandy spent 13 dimes on baseball cards. All in all, how much money did Sandy spend?

____

EXERCISE NO. 15

While digging through his clothes for ice cream money, Jason found 3 pennies in his shirt, and 7 pennies in his jacket. How much money did Jason find?

Sandy got 13 pennies and 14 dimes shining shoes, and in her tip jar found 5 dimes and 8 quarters. How much money did Sandy get?

Jason got 15 dimes for watering plants, and 16 nickels for washing clothes. How much money does Jason have?

COUNTING BILLS

Directions: Count the bills and write your answer in the space provided.

EXERCISE NO. 16

1)      $ ______

2)     $ ______

3)       $ ______

4)      $ ______

5)      $ ______

6)       $ ______

7)       $ ______

EXERCISE NO. 17

1)    $ _______

2)     $ _______

3)      $ _______

4)     $ _______

5)       $ _______

6)       $ _______

7)        $ _______

EXERCISE NO. 18

1)  $ ____

2)  $ ____

3)  $ ____

4)  $ ____

5) 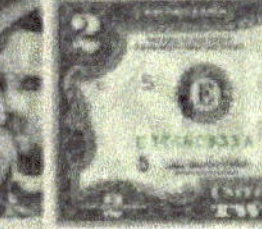 $ ____

6)  $ ____

7)  $ ____

1)  $ _______

2)  $ _______

3)  $ _______

4)  $ _______

5)  $ _______

6)  $ _______

7)  $ _______

1) 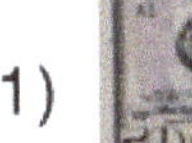 $ ______

2)  $ ______

3)  $ ______

4)  $ ______

5)  $ ______

6)  $ ______

7)  $ ______

EXERCISE NO. 21

1)  $ _______

2)  $ _______

3)  $ _______

4)  $ _______

5)  $ _______

6)  $ _______

7)  $ _______

8)  $ _______

1)        $ _______

2)       $ _______

3)      $ _______

4)       $ _______

5)     $ _______

6)       $ _______

7)        $ _______

1)  $ ______

2)  $ ______

3)  $ ______

4)  $ ______

5)  $ ______

6)  $ ______

7)  $ ______

EXERCISE NO. 24

1)       $ _______

2)      $ _______

3)     $ _______

4)     $ _______

5)     $ _______

6)       $ _______

7)        $ _______

8)    $ _______

EXERCISE NO. 25

1)  $ _______

2)  $ _______

3)  $ _______

4)  $ _______

5)  $ _______

6)  $ _______

7)  $ _______

EXERCISE NO. 26

1)  $ _______

2)  $ _______

3)  $ _______

4)  $ _______

5)  $ _______

6)  $ _______

EXERCISE NO. 27

1)       $ _________

2)      $ _________

3)       $ _________

4)       $ _________

5)       $ _________

6)        $ _________

EXERCISE NO. 28

1)  $ _______

2)  $ _______

3)  $ _______

4)  $ _______

5)  $ _______

6) 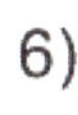 $ _______

EXERCISE NO. 29

1) 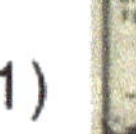       $ ______

2)        $ ______

3)       $ ______

4)           $ ______

5)         $ ______

6)          $ ______

7)      $ ______

1)       $ _______

2)       $ _______

3)        $ _______

4)      $ _______

5)         $ _______

6)       $ _______

7)     $ _______

COUNTING BILLS AND COINS

Directions: Count the bills and coins and write your answer in the space provided.

EXERCISE NO. 31

1)      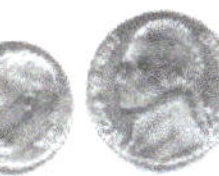 $ ______

2)      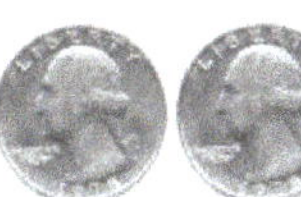 $ ______

3) 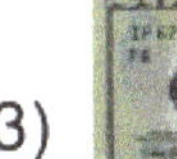       $ ______

4)        $ ______

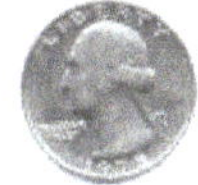  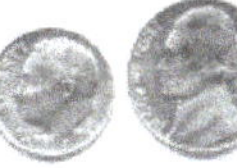   

5)         $ ______

EXERCISE NO. 32

1)       $ ______

2)         $ ______

3)        $ ______

4)        $ ______

5) 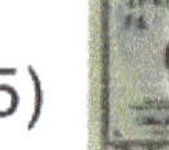        $ ______

EXERCISE NO. 33

1)       $ _______

2)        $ _______

3)        $ _______

4)        $ _______

5)        $ _______

EXERCISE NO. 34

1)  $ ______

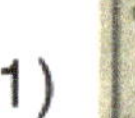     

2)       $ ______

3)       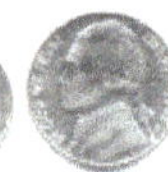  $ ______

4)         $ ______

5)        $ ______

EXERCISE NO. 35

1) 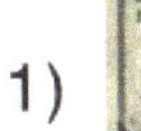        $ _______

2)        $ _______

  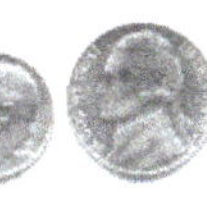   

3)         $ _______

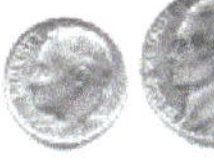 

4)         $ _______

5)         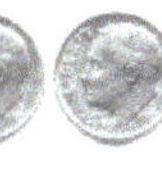 $ _______

1)       $ _______

2)        $ _______

3)        $ _______

4)        $ _______

5)         $ _______

EXERCISE NO. 37

1)       $ ______

2)       $ ______
   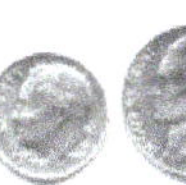 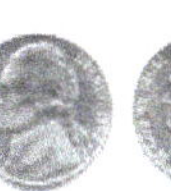 

3)        $ ______

4)        $ ______
    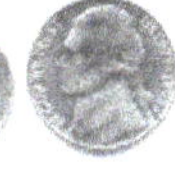

5)        $ ______

1)    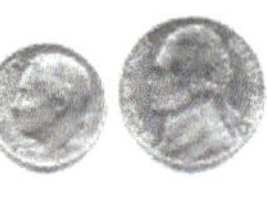   $ _______

2)       $ _______

3)       $ _______

 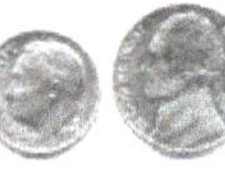 

4)       $ _______

5)         $ _______

EXERCISE NO. 39

1) 
 $ ______

2)  $ ______

3)  $ ______

4) 
 $ ______

5)  $ ______

EXERCISE NO. 40

1)       $ ______

   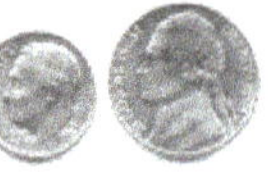 

2)       $ ______

3)         $ ______

4)        $ ______

5)        $ ______

EXERCISE NO. 1

1) Sally has 11 dimes and 5 quarters. All in all, how much money does Sally have?

235 cents

2) Sara sold lemonade in her neighborhood. She got 7 pennies on Saturday and 12 pennies on Sunday. What amount of money did Sara receive?

19 cents

3) When Benny was visited by the toothfairy, he received 16 each of dimes, pennies, and quarters. How much money did the toothfairy leave Benny?

576 cents

4) Jason got 13 pennies and 14 dimes shining shoes, and in his tip jar found
4 dimes and 2 quarters. How much money did Jason get?

243 cents

5) On Monday, Melanie spent 3 quarters playing pinball. The next day, she spent
16 quarters on pinball. What was the total amount Melanie spent playing pinball?

475 cents

6) While digging through her clothes for ice cream money, Joan found 14
quarters in her pants, and 18 quarters in her shirt. How much money

800 cents

7) As Sam was searching through his couch cushions, he found 14 dimes,
and 18 quarters in the couch. How much money in total does Sam have?

590 cents

8) On Friday, Sally spent 3 nickels on ice cream. The next day, Sally spent
18 pennies on baseball cards. All in all, how much money did Sally spend?

33 cents

9) Jessica found 17 nickels, 4 dimes, and 18 quarters in her house,
and found 6 dimes in her piggybank. How much money did Jessica find?

635 cents

1) When Sandy was visited by the toothfairy, she received 2 each of pennies,
dimes, and nickels. How much money did the toothfairy leave Sandy?

32 cents

2) Sam found 13 pennies, 18 dimes, and 17 quarters in his house,
and found 15 dimes in his piggybank. How much money did Sam find?

768 cents

3) Tom got 2 dimes for washing clothes, and 18 nickels for
watering plants. How much money does Tom have?

110 cents

4) As Joan was searching through her couch cushions, she found 7 pennies,
and 13 dimes in the couch. How much money in total does Joan have?

137 cents

5) Alyssa got 2 nickels and 15 quarters shining shoes, and in her tip jar found
12 quarters and 8 dimes. How much money did Alyssa get?

765 cents

6) Alyssa sold lemonade in her neighborhood. She got 2 pennies on Saturday
and 3 pennies on Sunday. What amount of money did Alyssa receive?

5 cents

EXERCISE NO. 6

7) On Friday, Sara spent 5 quarters on ice cream. The next day, Sara spent 17 dimes on baseball cards. All in all, how much money did Sara spend?

295 cents

8) On Tuesday, Jason spent 4 nickels playing pinball. The next day, he spent 13 nickels on pinball. What was the total amount Jason spent playing pinball?

85 cents

9) Jason has 3 pennies and 2 quarters. All in all, how much money does Jason have?

53 cents

EXERCISE NO. 7

1) On Friday, Keith spent 3 dimes on ice cream. The next day, Keith spent 15 quarters on baseball cards. All in all, how much money did Keith spend?

405 cents

2) Sally got 3 nickels for washing clothes, and 12 pennies for mowing lawns. How much money does Sally have?

27 cents

3) Fred sold lemonade in his neighborhood. He got 6 pennies on Saturday and 11 pennies on Sunday. What amount of money did Fred receive?

17 cents

EXERCISE NO. 8

4) As Tom was searching through his couch cushions, he found 6 dimes, and 2 quarters in the couch. How much money in total does Tom have?

110 cents

5) When Alyssa was visited by the toothfairy, she received 14 each of dimes, pennies, and nickels. How much money did the toothfairy leave Alyssa?

224 cents

6) While digging through her clothes for ice cream money, Sally found 7 pennies in her shorts, and 14 pennies in her jacket. How much money did Sally find?

21 cents

EXERCISE NO. 9

7) Jessica has 18 quarters and 15 nickels. All in all, how much money does Jessica have?

525 cents

8) Benny got 16 nickels and 2 pennies shining shoes, and in his tip jar found 8 pennies and 12 dimes. How much money did Benny get?

210 cents

9) Mary found 14 pennies, 17 dimes, and 4 nickels in her house, and found 18 dimes in her piggybank. How much money did Mary find?

384 cents

EXERCISE NO. 10

1) As Alyssa was searching through her couch cushions, she found 18 nickels, and 17 pennies in the couch. How much money in total does Alyssa have?

107 cents

2) Dan sold lemonade in his neighborhood. He got 4 pennies on Saturday and 9 pennies on Sunday. What amount of money did Dan receive?

13 cents

3) Sally found 3 dimes, 8 pennies, and 9 quarters in her house, and found 7 pennies in her piggybank. How much money did Sally find?

270 cents

EXERCISE NO. 11

4) Melanie got 16 dimes for washing clothes, and 13 nickels for mowing lawns. How much money does Melanie have?

225 cents

5) While digging through her clothes for ice cream money, Alyssa found 11 nickels in her pants, and 13 nickels in her jacket. How much money did Alyssa find?

120 cents

6) Mike got 12 pennies and 14 dimes shining shoes, and in his tip jar found 9 dimes and 17 quarters. How much money did Mike get?

667 cents

EXERCISE NO. 12

7) On Sunday, Joan spent 18 dimes playing pinball. The next day, she spent 15 dimes on pinball. What was the total amount Joan spent playing pinball?

330 cents

8) On Friday, Tom spent 17 pennies on ice cream. The next day, Tom spent 13 nickels on baseball cards. All in all, how much money did Tom spend?

82 cents

9) When Benny was visited by the toothfairy, he received 15 each of dimes, quarters, and nickels. How much money did the toothfairy leave Benny?

600 cents

EXERCISE NO. 13

1) As Sally was searching through her couch cushions, she found 11 pennies, and 12 quarters in the couch. How much money in total does Sally have?

311 cents

2) When Tim was visited by the toothfairy, he received 6 each of nickels, pennies, and dimes. How much money did the toothfairy leave Tim?

96 cents

3) Melanie has 16 pennies and 13 nickels. All in all, how much money does Melanie have?

81 cents

4) Nancy sold lemonade in her neighborhood. She got 17 nickels on Saturday and 10 nickels on Sunday. What amount of money did Nancy receive?

135 cents

5) On Wednesday, Dan spent 16 quarters playing pinball. The next day, he spent 4 quarters on pinball. What was the total amount Dan spent playing pinball?

500 cents

6) On Friday, Sandy spent 3 quarters on ice cream. The next day, Sandy spent 13 dimes on baseball cards. All in all, how much money did Sandy spend?

205 cents

EXERCISE NO. 15

7) While digging through his clothes for ice cream money, Jason found 3 pennies in his shirt, and 7 pennies in his jacket. How much money did Jason find?

10 cents

8) Sandy got 13 pennies and 14 dimes shining shoes, and in her tip jar found 5 dimes and 8 quarters. How much money did Sandy get?

403 cents

9) Jason got 15 dimes for watering plants, and 16 nickels for washing clothes. How much money does Jason have?

230 cents

EXERCISE NO. 16

1) $ 67

2) $ 66

3) $ 62

4) $ 61

5) $ 51

6) $ 42

7) $ 107

1) $ 66
2) $ 71
3) $ 72
4) $ 76
5) $ 82
6) $ 126
7) $ 172

1) $ 20
2) $ 35
3) $ 29
4) $ 21
5) $ 26
6) $ 34
7) $ 24

1) $ 321
2) $ 291
3) $ 272
4) $ 221
5) $ 191
6) $ 191
7) $ 413

1) $ 141
2) $ 81
3) $ 152
4) $ 131
5) $ 91
6) $ 161
7) $ 133

1) $ 37
2) $ 46
3) $ 62
4) $ 47
5) $ 56
6) $ 52
7) $ 38
8) $ 36

1) $ 26
2) $ 31
3) $ 33
4) $ 35
5) $ 28
6) $ 34
7) $ 32

1) $ 219
2) $ 217
3) $ 127
4) $ 224
5) $ 232
6) $ 229
7) $ 239

1) $ 240
2) $ 150
3) $ 140
4) $ 145
5) $ 140
6) $ 160
7) $ 245
8) $ 135

EXERCISE NO. 25

1) $ 140
2) $ 235
3) $ 165
4) $ 140
5) $ 235
6) $ 170
7) $ 260

EXERCISE NO. 26

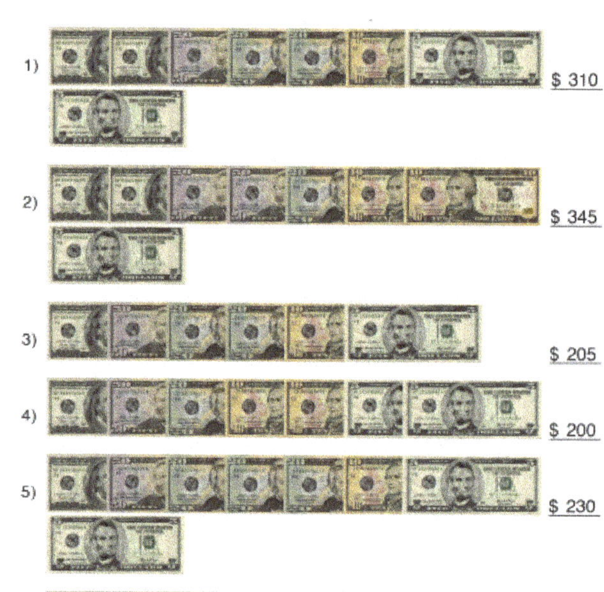

1) $ 310
2) $ 345
3) $ 205
4) $ 200
5) $ 230
6) $ 185

EXERCISE NO. 27

1) $ 241
2) $ 136
3) $ 156
4) $ 247
5) $ 171
6) $ 267

EXERCISE NO. 28

1) $ 60
2) $ 55
3) $ 44
4) $ 69
5) $ 67
6) $ 38

1) $ 125
2) $ 121
3) $ 120
4) $ 136
5) $ 129
6) $ 132
7) $ 118

1) $ 154
2) $ 145
3) $ 254
4) $ 153
5) $ 166
6) $ 243
7) $ 133

1) $ 36.56

2) $ 41.81

3) $ 46.46

4) $ 57.77

5) $ 42.09

1) $ 62.62

2) $ 36.57

3) $ 57.11

4) $ 56.62

5) $ 58.07

1) $ 133.06

2) $ 123.06

3) $ 226.56

4) $ 128.11

5) $ 116.63

1) $ 132.22

2) $ 126.32

3) $ 117.22

4) $ 126.32

5) $ 131.52

1) $ 117.27

2) $ 232.22

3) $ 227.16

4) $ 117.21

5) $ 126.56

1) $ 35.15

2) $ 23.80

3) $ 23.80

4) $ 34.80

5) $ 30.45

<table>
<tr><td>

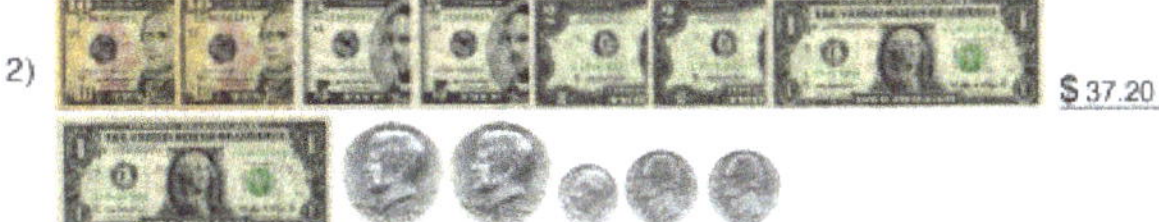
1) $ 28.65

2) $ 37.20

3) $ 21.65

4) $ 35.25

5) $ 19.70

</td><td>

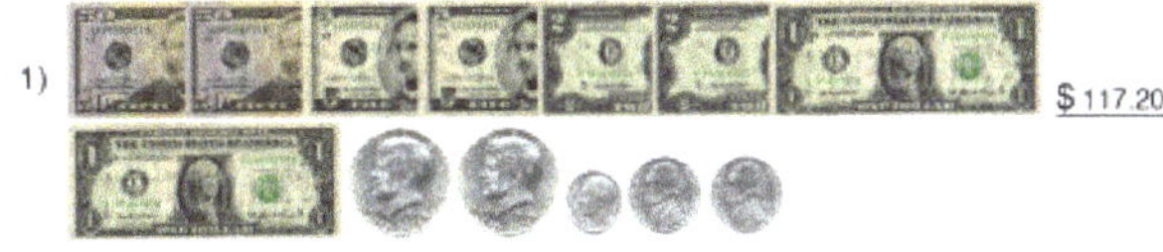
1) $ 117.20

2) $ 64.75

3) $ 115.70

4) $ 112.15

5) $ 59.80

</td></tr>
<tr><td>

1) $ 323.45

2) $ 268.85

3) $ 177.85

4) $ 173.65

5) $ 168.40

</td><td>

1) $ 135.30

2) $ 222.95

3) $ 119.70

4) $ 219.75

5) $ 234.65

</td></tr>
</table>

Visit

BABY PROFESSOR
EDUCATION KIDS

www.BabyProfessorBooks.com

to download Free Baby Professor eBooks
and view our catalog of new and exciting
Children's Books